Lives and Times

William Wrigley, Jr.

The Founder of Wrigley's Gum

M.C. Hall

Heinemann Library
Chicago, Illinois

Customer Service 888-454-2279
Visit our website at www.heinemannlibrary.com

Designed by Richard Parker and Maverick Design
Photo research by Julie Laffin
Printed and bound in China by South China Printing Company Limited

09 08 07 06 05
10 9 8 7 6 5 4 3 2 1

Library of Congress Cataloging-in-Publication Data
Hall, Margaret, 1947-
William Wrigley, Jr. and the beginning of Wrigley's chewing gum / M.C. Hall.
p. cm. -- (Lives and times)
Includes bibliographical references and index.
ISBN 1-4034-6347-6 (lib. bdg.) -- ISBN 1-4034-6361-1 (pbk.)
1. Wrigley, William, 1861-1932--Juvenile literature. 2. Businessmen--United States--Biography--Juvenile literature. 3. Wm. Wrigley Jr. Company--History--Juvenile literature. 4. Chewing gum industry--United States--History--Juvenile literature. I. Title. II. Series: Lives and times (Des Plaines, Ill.)
HD9970.5.C454W75 2005
338.7'6646--dc22

2004021938

Acknowledgments
The author and publishers are grateful to the following for permission to reproduce copyright material:
p. 4 Andrew E. Cook; pp. 5, 11, 21 Catalina Island Museum; p. 6 Hulton Archive/Getty Images; p. 7 Museum of the City of New York/Corbis; pp. 8, 23 Hulton Archive/Getty Images; p. 9 Bettmann/Corbis; pp. 10, 17 William Wrigley, Jr. Company; pp. 12, 24 Corbis; pp. 13, 14, 15 Mary Evans Picture Library; p. 16 Kit Kittle/Corbis; p. 18 Richard Cummins/Corbis; p. 19 Underwood & Underwood/Corbis; p. 20 Macduff Everton/Corbis; p. 22 Dallas and John Heaton/Corbis; p. 25 Wrigley Mansion Club Archives; p. 26 Janet Lankford Moran/Heinemann Library; p. 27 © Peter Jordan Photography

Cover photograph by The Granger Collection

Cover and interior icons Janet Lankford Moran/Heinemann Library

Every effort has been made to contact copyright holders of any material reproduced in this book. Any omissions will be rectified in subsequent printings if notice is given to the publishers.

Some words are shown in bold, **like this**. You can find out what they mean by looking in the glossary.

Contents

A Sticky Treat

Chewing gum has been around for thousands of years. For a long time, gum was made from things like **sap** and wax. It didn't always taste good. Today gum is sweet and tastes much better.

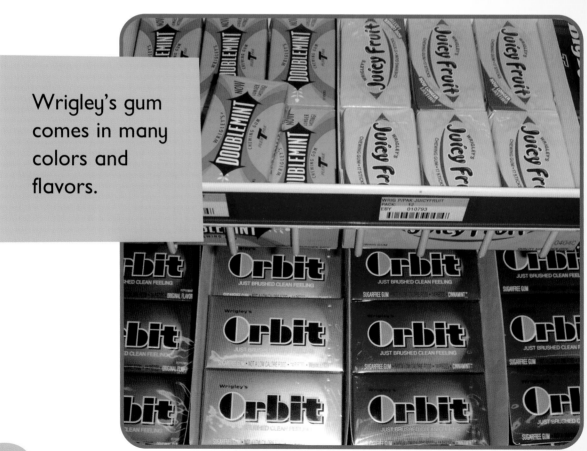

Wrigley's gum comes in many colors and flavors.

William Wrigley, Jr. was good at selling things. At first he sold other people's **products**. Then he started one of the biggest chewing gum **companies** in the world.

This is William Wrigley, Jr. in 1919.

The Early Years

William Wrigley, Jr. was born in Philadelphia, Pennsylvania, on September 30, 1861. He was one of nine children. William's father owned a soap **factory**.

This painting shows Philadelphia in the 1860s.

Newsboys sold newspapers on the streets.

When William was 11 years old, he ran away from home. He sold newspapers to earn money, and slept on the streets. When winter came, William went back home.

At Work in the Factory

William went back to school. But he soon got into trouble and was thrown out of school. His father was angry. He made William work in the soap **factory**.

At that time, there were many factories that made soap.

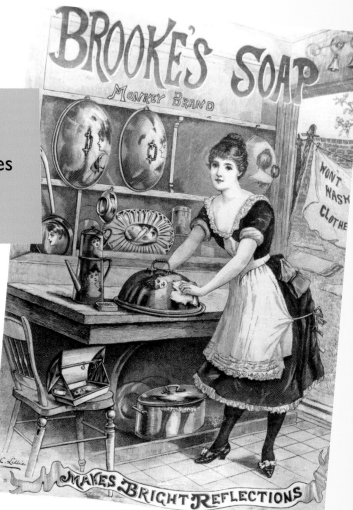

William's father gave him one of the worst jobs in the factory. He had to stir large pots of boiling soap. William wanted to sell soap, not make it.

Selling Soap

When William was 13 years old, his father agreed to let him sell soap. William became a **salesperson**. He traveled long distances by horse and wagon to visit his **customers**.

This is what Wrigley's soap looked like when William was selling it.

William did well and found new customers for his father's soap. In 1885 he married Ada Foote. William and Ada had two children, Dorothy and Philip. The family moved to Chicago, Illinois in 1891.

This is Ada when she was older.

Changing Products

William had an idea to sell more soap. He gave free **baking powder** to **customers**. Soon people wanted to buy baking powder more than they wanted soap.

William started selling baking powder.

William liked the idea of giving something away. He gave two packages of chewing gum to anyone who bought his baking powder. People wanted more gum. William decided to sell chewing gum.

This is an **advertisement** for gum in the 1920s.

On His Own

In the United States, there were already some **companies** that sold chewing gum. One of the largest companies offered William a job. William said no. He wanted to work on his own.

William wanted to sell gum in many different flavors.

William didn't make his gum himself. Instead, he paid another company to make his **products**. However, William had his name put on every package of gum.

Prizes for Buyers

Storekeepers who sold Wrigley's gum were given prizes. They could choose from a variety of things, such as clocks, flags, pens, and cameras. This made the storekeepers sell more gum.

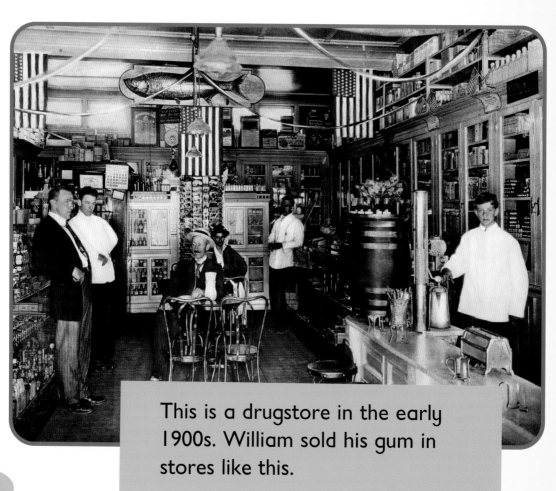

This is a drugstore in the early 1900s. William sold his gum in stores like this.

People started asking for Wrigley's gum by name. In 1911 William bought the **company** that made his gum. He gave it a new name—the William Wrigley, Jr. Company.

Wrigley's Mile-Long Sign stretches beside some railroad tracks.

A Growing Business

William's **company** did very well and he became rich. He liked to buy things that interested him. In 1915 William **invested** in the Chicago Cubs baseball team.

This is Wrigley Field where the Chicago Cubs play. It was named for William Wrigley in 1926.

In 1919 William bought Catalina Island, off the coast of California. He built a baseball field there. The Chicago Cubs sometimes used this field for practice.

Catalina Island

William spent a lot of money **improving** Catalina Island. He paid to build roads, hotels, and water pipes. He also bought two large ships. He sold tickets so people could visit the island.

Today, Catalina Island is a very popular place to take a vacation.

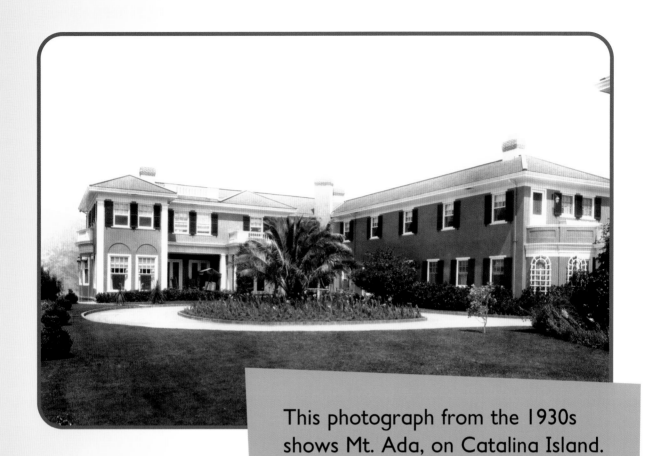

This photograph from the 1930s shows Mt. Ada, on Catalina Island.

William built a house on Catalina Island. He named the house for his wife, Ada. He also named a mountain on the island for her. The Wrigleys stayed in the house when they visited Catalina.

The Wrigley Building

In 1920 William built a new building for his **company**. At the time, the Wrigley Building was one of the tallest in Chicago. It was different because it was shaped like a triangle.

The Wrigley Building still stands in Chicago.

William Wrigley's son, Philip, started to run the company in 1925.

William ran the company for another five years. By then, the William Wrigley, Jr. Company had **factories** in the United States, Canada, and Australia.

The Later Years

William and Ada spent part of each winter in Phoenix, Arizona. In 1929 William built a big house there. It was a 50th wedding anniversary gift for Ada.

Here are William and Ada in 1929.

The Wrigley **Mansion** was huge. William owned four other houses that were even bigger. He and Ada only used the Phoenix house for a few months of each year.

The Wrigley Mansion in Phoenix had 12 bathrooms and 11 fireplaces.

More About William

William Wrigley, Jr. died on January 26, 1932. He was buried on Catalina Island. Later his body was moved to Glendale, California. Today his **company headquarters** is still in Chicago.

Today William Wrigley's gum is popular all over the world.

This is the Wrigley Mansion Club in Phoenix.

People can learn more about William by visiting the Wrigley **Mansion** in Phoenix, Arizona. The house is now a club. Members pay $10 a year. The money helps local people and groups.

Fact File

- When William first came to Chicago, he only had $32. Later, he was a rich man. Wrigley's gum only cost five cents a pack, but the **company** made millions of dollars.

- In 1915 William had Mother Goose rhymes rewritten to **advertise** Wrigley's gum. He gave away fourteen million copies of the book.

- In 1924 the William Wrigley, Jr. Company was the first to give all its workers Saturdays off.

- The William Wrigley, Jr. Company is still owned by the Wrigley family. William's great-grandson is now company president.

Timeline

1861	William Wrigley, Jr. is born in Philadelphia, Pennsylvania
1873	William starts to work in his father's soap **factory**
1874	William becomes a traveling **salesperson**
1885	William marries Ada Foote
1891	William moves to Chicago, Illinois
1911	William buys the Zeno Manufacturing Company. He changes its name to the William Wrigley, Jr. Company.
1919	William buys Catalina Island
1920	Work begins to build the Wrigley Building in Chicago
1925	William turns the company over to his son, Philip
1926	The Chicago baseball park where the Cubs play is named "Wrigley Field"
1932	William Wrigley, Jr. dies in Phoenix, Arizona

Glossary

advertisements signs, newspaper stories, and other things that tell or show people about products

baking powder white powder used in baking and cooking

company group of people who makes money by selling things

customers people who buy a product

factory building in which things are made

headquarters place from which a business is run

improving making something better

investor person who buys something in order to make money out of it

mansion very large, fancy house

product something that is made

salesperson someone who earns money by selling a company's products or services

sap liquid found inside trees and other plants

More Books to Read

Landau, Elaine. *Chewing Gum: A Sticky Treat.* Vero Beach, FL: Rourke, 2001.

Marsh, Carole. *William Wrigley, Jr.: Chewing Gum Giant.* Peachtree, GA: Gallopade Publishing Group, 1998.

Swain, Ruth Freeman. *How Sweet It Is (and Was): The History of Candy.* New York, NY: Holiday House, 2003.

Wardlaw, Lee. *Bubblemania: A Chewy History of Bubble Gum.* New York, NY: Aladdin, 1997.

Index